# Catherine of Valois:
## The Tudor Queen Ahead of Her Time

## By K. Lee Pelt
### AKA The Snarky History Nerd

Snarky Mini Bios: The War of The Roses
Volume 1

# COPYRIGHT PAGE

Catherine of Valois: The Tudor Queen Ahead of Her Time by K. Lee

Copyright © 2022 K. Lee Pelt.

First Edition 2022

This book is dedicated to my wonderful
parents, Dave and Cindy. Through thick
and thin, they have always unconditionally
supported and loved me. I would not be where
I am today without them.

# Table of Contents

# Introduction

It has been 400 years since the death of the last Tudor monarch; yet, it is still one of the most famous dynasties in history. You could walk down the street and ask a random person if they can name at least one medieval monarch, you can almost guarantee that Henry VIII or Elizabeth I would be included in the list, if not the entire list. The decisions that the Tudor monarchs made changed not only British history but world history as well (as the first colonization projects outside of the British Isles were authorized under Elizabeth I).

Looking back, one would assume that the Tudor dynasty was inevitable. How could it not be? They were notorious and changed so much. The reality was the exact opposite. When Henry VII was born, the fact that he would one day become king was ridiculous. And frankly, that his parents married and conceived him was an anomaly (and not just because Margaret Beaufort was only thirteen when she gave birth. That fact never gets less gross or horrifying). The road to the Tudors taking the throne started with a mostly forgotten Queen of England: Catherine of Valois.

Catherine of Valois lived during one of the most volatile times in French and English medieval history and her impact reached far beyond what anyone who knew her would have expected. She was a key figure in the Hundred Years' War, as the daughter of the French king and wife of the English king. She was the mother of the king who started the War of the Roses. And finally, she was the grandmother of the king who started the most notorious dynasty in English history, the Tudors. And without her, these events would have looked very different, or frankly, not even happened.

To be clear, I am not just referring to the fact that biologically, if she did not give birth to Edmund Tudor, Henry VII would not have existed. Her impact goes beyond that. In order for the Tudor dynasty to come into power, the stars had to align in a very specific way. And Catherine was essentially that first star that all the other stars had to align to. She was the first domino, so to speak. Even when she had the least power, the decisions that she made paved the way for the events that would unfold in the years following her death that changed English history forever.

This book provides a look at Catherine of Valois's life and impact on history. It will be snarky and there will be cursing. All of the sources that I used to collect my information will be in "Appendix C: Sources and Further Reading". I highly recommend that you check out these sources as they are fantastic. Each chapter begins with a section of "The Snarky Poem on the Life of Catherine of Valois." The full poem can be found in the epilogue. Enjoy.

# Baby French Princess

Once upon a time

In the land of croissants, pastries, and escargot,

There was a little princess

Hidden away as the shit hit the fan...

Knees sore, the young girl tried to remain perfectly still. Her whole body shakes with the effort. Although only a ward of the convent, she was expected to complete all of the rituals to perfection. No movement was allowed during prayer, no matter how many hours they remained on their knees praying. At his moment, Catherine forgot what she was supposed to be praying about and began praying that she would not be stuck here her whole life.

※※※※※

Growing up as a French princess may seem like a dream come true to most, but for Catherine of Valois, it was, in many ways, a living nightmare. France, to put it simply, was a hot mess. There was a civil war in France raging. England took advantage of the chaos and restarted the Hundred Years War. This was

Catherine's world, especially since her father was the French King, Charles VI.

Charles VI started his reign (after a long corrupt regency) with the nickname "The Beloved." The French public adored him and were riding high, which of course, meant that his fall was long and hard (that's what she said). In 1392, only four years into his reign, Charles VI suffered the first of many episodes of psychosis. Sometimes, he became violent (such as when he slaughtered members of his army, thinking they were the enemy). Other times, he became harmlessly delusional (such as when he thought he was made of glass and could shatter at any moment). It quickly became clear that he could not run the country nor was it safe to be around him. This was one of the reasons why Catherine spent the majority of her childhood living in her sister's convent.

Isabeau of Bavaria, the Queen of France, became the most prominent regent during Charles VI's periods of insanity. This, of course, also made her an easy target for... well... everybody. A long-standing tradition in European countries was to blame the wife for the husband's faults, especially when that husband is King and to blame him was treason. But (because women did not matter) to blame the Queen was not treason, so everything was her fault. (My eyes just rolled so hard I pulled a muscle). Keeping to this "fun" tradition, the nobles blamed Isabeau for everything. Literally.

At this point, the nobles sought to grab power for themselves, like sharks smelling blood in the water. Two factions, the Armagnacs and Burgudians, formed and began an all-out civil war. Isabeau did her best to appease each side (while giving birth and raising TWELVE children) but it often backfired. When she was close with the Armagnac side, there were rumors that she was having an affair with the leader, the Duke of Orleans. When she sided with the Burgudians, they accused her of flip flopping. No matter what she did, each side blamed her for whatever went wrong. Due to the propaganda, she has gone down in history as one of the worst French Queens, along with Marie Antoinette and Catherine de' Medici. It was the Treaty of Troyes that ultimately dug her grave in history; it also sealed her daughter's, Catherine of Valois, fate.

# The Shining New Queen Consort of England

The golden princess stands behind the drawbridge.

Her future is just on the other side.

She looks over her shoulder

At the illusion of safety and home

That she was leaving behind.

She jumps

As the drawbridge creaks open.

The choice is made for her.

There is no way to go but forward.

She squares her shoulders,

Head held high.

When the drawbridge lands with a thud

She steps forward,

Ready to take on the world

And immediately

Gets hit in the face with a giant ball of horse manure...

A small group of people gathered in front of a convent near Troyes, France, waiting impatiently for the English king to arrive. The beautiful young woman at the center of the group was not only impatient but nervous. Her voluminous sleeves hid her shaking hands. She straightened her shoulders, raising her chin as though in defiance, if only to prevent the heavy cone shaped headdress from falling off of the intricate hairstyle that her ladies-in-waiting had forced her dirty blonde hair into that morning.

You would think that having her parents standing by her side would be a comfort in this moment of significant change but they were essentially strangers to her. In fact, the familiarity of the convent behind her provided more comfort than her parents' presence at that moment. While this was not the convent she was raised in by her older sister, Marie, it was the environment she knew. It had been years since she had seen her father, his madness making it unsafe to be around him. And her mother barely had time to check in on her remaining children while trying to run a fractured county. The young woman understood. She really did. But the emotional neglect still hurts. So she found little comfort in either of their presences.

At first, she could only see a speck in the distance, but soon, she could make out the royal procession in the distance. Instinctively, she knew that this w as the man that she was waiting for. The man that she would marry. The man who would make her Queen of not just England but also France. A bittersweet notion, as that was her brother's birthright. She pushed those ugly thoughts aside, because if nothing else, Catherine of Valois knew her role and she was determined to execute it to the best of her ability.

❈❈❈❈❈

At eighteen years old, Catherine was ready to be married. She, like all other high-born women, knew that her role was to marry for the benefit of her family. Her future husband, Henry V, had been a potential match for her for years; however, it was the French defeat at Agincourt that finally made it happen. Henry V had a real chance at conquering France, and in a failed attempt to cease the bloodshed, Charles VI and Isabeau signed the Treaty of Troyes. This treaty stipulated that Henry V would marry Catherine and become Charles

VI's heir, making him the future King of France. Of course, this meant that Catherine's brother, Charles VII, was removed from the line of succession. To be clear, it was generally a really bad idea to remove your own son as your heir. It usually led to way too much bloodshed.

Authors, such as Shakespeare, romanticized the moment that Henry V and Catherine of Valois first saw each other. There is no doubt that Henry V and Catherine were a very good-looking pair. There was likely an attraction, especially since Catherine was pregnant pretty much right away. The "love at first sight" storyline was a hell of a lot better than the reality, which was Henry V seeing Catherine and thinking some version of "damn, she is hot" or "I could sleep with that in exchange for France." At the end of the day, this was a political match, not a love match, no matter what anyone said.

While the love story was likely fictional (likely by the Tudors, who descended from Catherine's second marriage), the wedding itself was certainly a great celebration. The marriage was a crucial part of the English (finally) claiming the French throne. Not to mention the fact that Henry was not getting any younger and his childless brother was the current heir to the throne.

While the marriage and treaty were basically a wet dream for Henry V, he immediately went back to war. This time, however, he rode to meet his brother-in-law in battle not as a usurper but as the rightful future King of France. At least legally. In an effort to support her new husband, Catherine followed his blood trail around France. Henry V and Catherine ended their "tour" of France (AKA invasion) in Paris around Christmas. After Christmas, they headed to England for Catherine's introduction to her new subjects, the English people.

Catherine's coronation finally took place in February, after Henry and Catherine arrived in England. It was a very lavish and celebrated event. Henry was at the height of his reign, having just won the most significant battle of his reign (the Battle of Agincourt) and securing the French throne which had been the English king's wet dream since William the Conqueror. His marriage to Catherine represented all of this success. It, of course, helped that she was beautiful and got pregnant weeks after her coronation.

# Everything Is Looking Up...

She sits on a golden throne

with golden beams of light

shimmering around her,

as she cradles her burgeoning belly

knowing that all of the future of her new nation

lay protected beneath her heart.

For once,

everything is secure;

everything is alright.

The stars have aligned,

she thought.

She ignores her crown slipping to the side

as the shadows creep in around the edges.

She just repeats to herself,

everything is fine;

everything is alright.

27

Seated in the royal carriage, utilizing her years of practice remaining completely still while praying for hours at the convent with her sister as the carriage bumped along the road to the Château de Vincennes. Her companions struggled to maintain their seats while she sustained her regal posture through every bump and jolt. As they get closer to their destination, she finds herself straining to see a glimpse of the Chateau or her husband or both. This was exactly where Catherine needed to be.

❊❊❊❊❊❊

Now pregnant, Catherine stayed in London as Henry went back on the road again. During their short trip to England, Thomas of Clarence (Henry V's brother and second-in-line for the throne) died in a critical battle in France. After raising funds to continue the war in France,

Henry headed back to France to continue asserting his claim to the French throne. This was the last time that Henry would set foot in England.

Catherine and Henry remained apart for approximately a year. During that time, Catherine gave birth to their only child, Henry VI. After recovering from the birth, Catherine joined Henry on his military campaign. They spent a little time together before Henry continued his "military defense" of France (still an invasion) and Catherine went to visit her parents.

Having spent most of the last several years on the battlefield, Henry's cause of death was anticlimactic. He caught dysentery, a disease commonly found on the battlefield, and died soon after. The primary symptom of dysentery was a shit ton of diarrhea (pun intended). So, Henry V basically shat himself to death.

As Henry V lay on his deathbed, he called his brothers to his side and made his final requests. Very specifically, Catherine was left out of these conversations. Not only did Henry not send for her (and she was close enough that she could have made it to his side), but he also removed any potential power that Catherine could have consolidated as Queen Mother. Once again, Catherine's future was determined without her being in the room.

# Dowager Queen

Shrouded in black,

That same golden princess,

Infant on hip,

Stood in front of her husband's tomb.

The large, cold, stone statue of the dead man

Staring down on them.

The only way her son will ever meet his father.

She feels the heat of the glares on her back,

From her new subjects.

She has gone from their Queen to their enemy.

She breathes,

The weight of the world on her shoulders

And whispers,

"Well, Bugger..."

It took all of her control but the young queen managed to hide her dismay in front of her father's court. The large pit that had formed in her stomach when she heard the news that her husband was dead only grew heavier with each step that she took to her private chambers. All of the ramifications raced through her mind, giving her a pounding headache. Onlookers saw none of this turmoil; the only sign of her distress was her shaking hands, which she skillfully hid in the large sleeves of her dress. She did not know what the future held for her, but Catherine of Valois knew that everything was about to change and with her luck, not for the better.

❋❋❋❋❋

Catherine accompanied her husband's body back to England, as was expected of her. With her husband dead, despite being French herself, she had no reason to remain in France. Her priority was now her son, Henry VI, the new King of England, and heir to the French throne. At this time, Henry VI had not seen his first birthday and would never meet his father, the great Henry V.

Catherine's financial and political situation was strained at this time. As the new Dowager Queen, her household was funded by the Dowager funds. This was normally not an issue (and the one thing that Henry V did for her on his deathbed was ensure that she would receive dowager funds); however, she was not the only Dowager Queen alive, which was unusual. Joan of Navarre, Henry IV's second wife and Henry V's stepmother, was still alive and recently "pardoned" from the witchcraft charges (a long story that mostly revolved around Henry V needing funds and Joan having the funds). Each Queen had their own household that needed to be funded with the same funds, which made things financial tight for both of them.

As the Queen Mother to the infant king, despite not being Regent, she was able to exert a certain level of power. Henry VI remained in her household for the next several years. Even as a toddler, there were certain governmental procedures that only the king could do, regardless of his age. Since Henry VI resided with Catherine for the beginning years of his life, Catherine remained part of the political court.

# Propaganda

The golden princess turned China doll

Gathering dust on the highest shelf

Only brought out to impress.

Then forgotten once again.

But when the lights are out

And the critical eyes are gone

The China doll dances

To the music that only she can hear

Until someone comes along

That hears it too.

The first time she was called "Her Majesty, the Dowager Queen", she almost did not realize that they were addressing her. So lost in the whirlwind of thoughts, she almost did not respond. Her hands, which seemed to perpetually be shaking at this point, hidden in her long sleeves, were the only outward sign of her distress. Her beautiful face remained serene as she swallowed back the nausea that clogged her throat. She was too young to be the Dowager Queen. Her bright shiny future as Queen Consort of England was supposed to still be in front of her. Instead, it was now part of her past. Her future seemed bleak, colorless, joyless. But Catherine knew, none of these thoughts could show. If they did, the court vultures would eat her alive.

From the get-go, Catherine was a propaganda tool for England. While Henry V's success in France was a point of pride for the English, war costs money and time. The more time and money Henry V spent on France took away from the time and money that he devoted to his English subjects. Catherine represented the success of the Hundred Years War and Henry V made sure to flaunt her while they were in England.

After Henry V's death, Catherine's role was significantly diminished. Her role as queen disappeared. While her son, Henry VI, lived with her for some of his childhood, she was not involved in important aspects of raising him, such as his education. The Regency Council treated her as an afterthought rather than a Queen Dowager. To the Regency Council, her only usefulness was her image. Her marriage to Henry V solidified the English claim on the French throne and her son was the current king. She could only ever be the Dowager Queen. To be anything else, would ruin the image that they needed her to maintain.

# Edmund Beaufort

The first one who came to dance

Appeared to be perfect.

Handsome and charming,

He bowed before the China doll as he asked her to
dance.

As they twirled around the dusty shelf,

She beams of joy,

Basking in the love showered upon her.

For the first time,

Things seem to be going her way.

It was on one of her few forays into court. These days, it was only when the loneliness grew unbearable that she dared face the viper pit that was court. One this one foray, she caught a glimpse of a handsome young man across the room. Maybe it was his handsomeness that caught her eye or that he turned out to be a Beaufort. Probably a little bit of both. Either way, she found herself drawn to him throughout her visit, like a moth to the flame. Catherine began to have dangerous thoughts about having a little slice of happiness for herself once again.

❊❊❊❊❊❊❊

Catherine's first foray into having a love life bit her in the ass. Catherine had grown up knowing that she would be a wife and mother.

When she married Henry V, she expected she would be Queen for years to come and have many children. Instead, she was a widow in her early twenties and had one child who she had less and less contact with. The Regency Council expected Catherine to sit down and shut up and stay in her lane as Dowager Queen. For the first time in her life, Catherine went for what she wanted, to be a wife and mother, regardless of the consequences.

The first man that Catherine courted was Edmund Beaufort. John of Gaunt, one of Edward III's surviving sons, created the Beaufort family name for his children with Kathryn Swynford. The children were born illegitimate but legitimized after John and Kathryn finally married. As the half-siblings to Henry IV, they were firmly entrenched in the

Royal Court. Edmund Beaufort was the fourth son of John Beaufort, the eldest son of the OG Beaufort siblings. As the fourth son, he did not expect to inherit anything and had to make his own way.

At this time, the Beaufort family was in a difficult position. Edmund's older brothers were prisons of war in France. His uncle, Cardinal Henry Beaufort, the Bishop of Winchester, had lost his powerful position on the Regency Council, with Humphrey of Gloucester winning the power struggle. Edmund sought to change his family's fortune by pursuing the Dowager Queen, Catherine of Valois.

Catherine, on her own, had very little power. She was French and England was waging a war against her brother, the French Dauphin. With no time to establish herself as an English Queen before Henry V's death, the English public regarded her as French and therefore an enemy. Her influence over her son was significantly limited. If she married a high-ranking Englishman, especially one as well connected as Edmund, she would be more trustworthy. Edmund and Catherine would have been a power couple, as the Dowager Queen and cousin to the King.

The possibility of a marriage between Edmund and Catherine terrified Humphrey of Gloucester. He had just won his political war with one Beaufort (Cardinal Henry Beaufort) and the primary Beaufort heirs (Edmund's older brothers) were prisoners of war. If Edmund married Catherine, he would rapidly gain power and that was a threat that Humphrey could not ignore.

The Regency Council passed a law that stated that any Dowager Queen could not remarry without the permission of the King. They were able to get away with putting this law in place because Joan of Navarre was still alive. However, this law was clearly meant for Catherine. There were significant ramifications for breaking the law. Any financial or political power gained by marrying Catherine disappeared and with it, so did Edmund.

# Mustache Twirling Villain

The door creaks open,

A gnarled, green hand sneaks through

Followed by its ugly face

With a crooked nose and bulging eyes

That darkened with malice at the very sight

Of the China doll glowing with happiness.

Rage had never been a huge part of her life. There were moments when she could remember being angry, but she had always pushed those feelings down. Anger would not have served her in those moments. And it would not serve her now; yet the rage boiled over. She could not contain it. At the sight of his gloating face, she just saw red, her blood boiling. Catherine vowed then and there to have her happily ever after, regardless of what that slimy toad had to say.

✴✴✴

There was no one who was as unlikable as Humphrey of Gloucester. As the youngest son of Henry IV, he was a powerful political player. However, he lacked the finesse to be very successful at it. In fact, he made more enemies than friends and was particularly vindictive.

Unfortunately, and frankly unfairly, Catherine was the target of much of his vindictive attacks.

While they never liked each other, prior to the Tudor scandal, their major conflict was over Humphrey's treatment of his wife, Jaqueline of Hainault. Jaqueline's first husband had been Catherine's older brother, John. Given Catherine's turbulent reception, Jaqueline was a breath of fresh air. She was one of the few connections that Catherine had to her birth family. So, it was really not surprising that Catherine took Jaqueline's side when Jacqueline and Humphrey's marriage exploded.

Jaqueline was her father's only legitimate heir, so she inherited Hainault, Holland, and Zeeland (medieval territories that are in the Netherlands and France today) upon his death. However, because she was a woman, her extended male relatives immediately jumped on her inheritance. She ended up in the English court, looking for support to take her inheritance back from her uncle, Phillip of Burgundy, and her maybe second husband, John IV of Brabant. Her marriage to John IV was potentially not legal as the Pope revoked the Papal Dispensation for their marriage at one point. Either way, the two men had scammed Jacqueline out her inheritance, and she was going to get it back.

Humphrey, ever the opportunist, took one look at Jacqueline and decided that he wanted her inheritance for himself. He charmed her, married her, and immediately attempted to reclaim her inheritance.

Now, marrying for money, land, and power was quite common. It was the basis for Catherine's marriage as well. That was never one of the many issues in Humphrey and Jacqueline's marriage. The issue was Humphrey's mistress, Eleanor Cobham.

Eleanor was a daughter of a knight who joined Jacqueline's ladies-in-waiting before her marriage to Humphrey. A few years into their marriage, Eleanor caught Humphrey's eye and they began a very public affair. Once it became clear that Humphrey would not be able to reclaim Jacqueline's inheritance, he very publicly spurned Jacqueline for Eleanor and got their marriage annulled to marry Eleanor.

As Jacqueline's sister-in-law two times over, Catherine sided with Jacqueline during this scandal. Truthfully, even if Jacqueline and Catherine had not been close, she still would have sided with her. The way Humphrey and

Eleanor flaunted their relationship was a slap in Jacqueline's face and very few people sided with Humphrey. For Catherine, however, her loyalty to Jacqueline had a high cost. It cost her the agency to move forward with her life.

# The Tudor Scandal

One more piece of joy ripped from her,

By the jackasses at court.

Never shall she marry,

They declare.

The China doll cracks and shatters,

As she reaches the end of her rope.

"Fuck you"

She roars,

Her middle finger in the air.

"Bugger you all."

These are the final words

Of the golden princess and the China doll.

They are dead and gone.

And all that is left is the rebel Queen.

Secure in her private chambers, her trembling hands cradled her burgeoning belly where her unborn child was safely secured. Years before, when she had been in this very same condition, she had been alone. No mother, no husband, and in a foreign land, she had felt so alone. Now, she knew what real loneliness felt like. But at this moment, she was not alone. A male hand reached around her and covered her trembling hands with his own, cradling her and their unborn child. She felt the warm chest of her husband against her back and she smiled. For the first time since leaving the convent all those years ago, Catherine was not alone.

Catherine decided that regardless of the consequences, she was going to get what she wanted. And what she wanted was a husband and a family. Due to the extreme punishment for any who dares to marry Catherine (AKA loss of money, power, and land), all of the eligible suitors ran for the hills. So, she turned her eyes to the unsuitable ones; specifically, a Welsh man who worked in her household, by the name of Owen Tudor. After all, according to legend, he did literally fall in her lap.

Legend has it that while dancing, he fell into her lap. This caught her eye (because how could she miss a grown man falling into her lap) and they soon began a romantic relationship. They married in secret and had four children. Only two of their children survived to adulthood, Edmund, and Jasper.

Catherine was able to keep the marriage secret by retiring from court when she became pregnant. Her illegal marriage to Owen was definitely public knowledge by her last pregnancy. Humphrey saw this as an opportunity to make Catherine miserable. His next move had tragic results.

Humphrey sent Catherine to Bermondsey Abbey for the remainder of her pregnancy. She was separated from her husband and children, which was not something she would willingly do. Her fifth pregnancy was a rough one physically, and her emotional turmoil did not help matters. Not only was she separated from her beloved family, but her mother had also just passed away. Overall, she was in physical and mental ill health by the time she arrived at the Abbey.

Catherine gave birth to her one and only daughter at the Abbey. There was very little record of the child, which likely indicated that the child died not long after her birth. Unfortunately, Catherine soon passed away as well. She never saw any of her children or her husband again.

# The Legacy of Catherine of Valois

The Rebel Queen is gone but not forgotten

As a comforting ghost to some

And a banshee to others.

Her legacy lives on

Through her precious family

In ways that anyone ever imagined.

At first glance, Catherine of Valois was a pretty average royal medieval woman. She was a French princess who married a king. Both her son and grandson became king. On its face, that legacy was very ordinary. It was the details that make it extraordinary.

Her parents were a Mad French King and a reviled Queen. Her childhood was dominated by a civil war and an English invasion (a traumatic childhood to say the least). While her reign as Queen Consort to Henry V was very short, Catherine literally made the English aristocracy's dreams come true by bringing all of France as her dowry AND immediately got pregnant with the heir to the throne. Her time as Dowager Queen was toxic (due to turds like Humphrey of Gloucester). While these things would have made her an interesting woman to study, it was her contribution to the Tudor dynasty that made her extraordinary.

In a normal world, being the grandmother of Henry VII was expected. Fathers and sons often shared first names, and he was named after her husband and son. Plus, as the Dowager Queen, her grandson was expected to become a king. Henry VII's father was one of Catherine's sons' children, but his father was Edmund Tudor, not Henry VI (cue the dramatic music).

For a variety of reasons, even though Catherine of Valois was his mother, Edmund Tudor was never in line for the throne. First off, his father, Owen Tudor, was Welsh. Not only was he Welsh, but Owen was the son of a Welsh rebel! Secondly, the marriage between Catherine and Owen was not entirely legal (because Humphrey of Gloucester was a vindictive jerk). They were forced to marry in secret, so there was little record of the actual marriage ceremony.

Upon Catherine's death, no one could have predicted that her second son would be the father of a king. In fact, after Edmund's own death, the idea that his son would one day be king was laughable. Henry VI and his own son, Edward of Lancaster, were alive and there were countless nobles who were ahead of Henry VII in the line of succession. Not to mention, Henry VII's only claim to the throne (which was very very thin) was through his mother, Margaret Beaufort, not Edmund. Even though he was half-brother to the English King, Edmund himself was French and Welsh with literally no English royal descent.

The only reason Edmund was able to marry Margaret Beaufort (a rich heiress who was cousin to the king) was because he was Henry VI's half-brother. Henry VI cared deeply for his mother. He took care of his half-brothers, which led to Edmund's marriage to Margaret. (That marriage is so gross. She was way too young at 12, even for the time.) Essentially, the only reason Henry VII existed was because of Catherine's most scandalous choice: her marriage to Owen Tudor.

One of the only times Catherine took control of her life (which frankly, she had very little agency for most of her life) was when she married Owen Tudor even though it was illegal. This moment of agency changed the course of history, although those changes did not happen until well after her death. If Owen had married anyone else, Edmund would have not married Margaret and Henry VII would never have been born.

# Epilogue

## The Snarky Poem of Catherine of Valois

Once upon a time

In the land of croissants, pastries, and escargot,

There was a little princess

Hidden away as the shit hit the fan...

૱

The golden princess stands behind the drawbridge.

Her future is just on the other side.

She looks over her shoulder

At the illusion of safety and home

That she was leaving behind.

She jumps

As the drawbridge creaks open.

The choice is made for her.

There is no way to go but forward.

She squares her shoulders,

Head held high.

When the drawbridge lands with a thud

She steps forward,

Ready to take on the world

And immediately

Gets hit in the face with a giant ball of crap...

⊂℞⊃

She sits on a golden throne

with golden beams of light

shimmering around her,

as she cradles her burgeoning belly

knowing that all of the future of her new nation

lay protected beneath her heart.

For once,

everything is secure;

everything is alright.

The stars have aligned,

she thought.

She ignores her crown slipping to the side

as the shadows creep in around the edges.

She just repeats to herself,

everything is fine;

everything is alright.

⛤

Shrouded in black,

That same golden princess,

Infant on hip,

Stood in front of her husband's tomb.

The large, cold, stone statue of the dead man

Staring down on them.

The only way her son will ever meet his father.

She feels the heat of the glares on her back,

From her new subjects.

She has gone from their Queen to their enemy.

She breathes,

The weight of the world on her shoulders

And whispers,

"Well, Fuck..."

ೲ

The golden princess turned China doll

Gathering dust on the highest shelf

Only brought out to impress.

Then forgotten once again.

But when the lights are out

And the critical eyes are gone

The China doll dances

To the music that only she can hear

Until someone comes along

That hears it too.

The first one who came to dance

Appeared to be perfect.

Handsome and charming,

He bowed before the China doll as he asked her to
dance.

As they twirled around the dusty shelf,

She beams of joy,

Basking in the love showered upon her.

For the first time,

Things seem to be going her way.

The door creaks open,

A gnarled, green hand sneaks through

Followed by its ugly face

With a crooked nose and bulging eyes

That darkened with malice at the very sight

Of the China doll glowing with happiness.

CƷ℟

One more piece of joy ripped from her,

By the jackasses at court.

Never shall she marry,

They declare.

The China doll cracks and shatters,

As she reaches the end of her rope.

"Fuck you"

She roars,

Her middle finger in the air.

"Fuck you all."

These are the final words

Of the golden princess and the China doll.

They are dead and gone.

And all that is left is the rebel Queen.

℥℥

The Rebel Queen is gone but not forgotten

As a comforting ghost to some

And a banshee to others.

Her legacy lives on

Through her precious family

In ways that anyone ever imagined.

# Appendix A

# What Happened to Everyone Else?

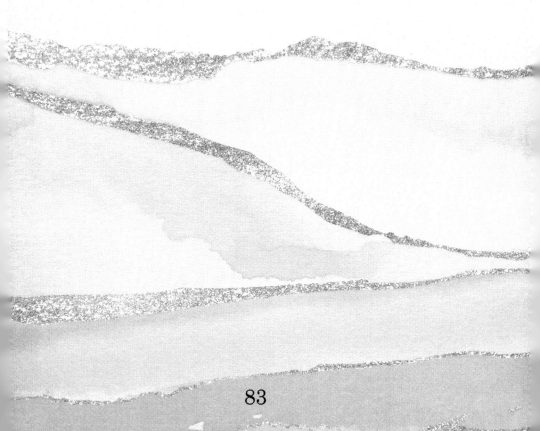

Unfortunately, Catherine's story ended far too young, but her friends and family continued on without her. This chapter provides a brief overview of what happened to some of the historical figures who took part in Catherine's journey.

### JACQUELINE OF HAINAULT

Jacqueline lost everything in the end. Phillip of Burgundy out maneuvered her politically and she ended up signing a treaty that essentially gave him control over everything. She had a short but happy final marriage before her death in 1434.

### HUMPHREY OF GLOUCESTER

Things went south for Humphrey after Catherine's death. Henry VI held Humphrey indirectly responsible for Catherine's death. It did not help that he arrested Owen behind Henry VI's back. With Henry VI old enough to make actual decisions, Humphrey rapidly lost political support. The final nail in his coffin came when his wife, Eleanor Cobham, was convicted of witchcraft. He died alone with no heirs.

## ELEANOR COBHAM

Eleanor and Humphrey's court was a lively and fun place. This changed after Catherine's death. As Humphrey's political star faded, Eleanor contacted two astrologers who predicted Henry VI's death. Word got back to Humphrey's enemies, and they manipulated the situation to accuse Eleanor of witchcraft. She was forcibly divorced from her husband and sent to live her days alone in exile.

## Owen Tudor

Immediately after Catherine's death, Humphrey secretly arrested Owen. He was held in the worst prison until Henry VI discovered that he was imprisoned and released him. Henry VI granted Owen a pension and lived comfortably for the rest of his life. He died in one of the early battles of the War of the Roses.

## Edmund Tudor

As the maternal half-brother of the reigning English King, Edmund was named Earl of Richmond and given lands worthy of his station. He was an advisor to Henry VI, who was his brother, although his primary duty was to be a liaison between the King and the Welsh. He married a wealthy heiress, Margaret Beaufort, when she was only 12 years old. This took place at the outbreak of the War of the Roses, and he insisted on consummating the marriage before leaving for battle, despite her young age. He died while in captivity within a year of the marriage. He never met his son, the future Henry VII.

### JASPER TUDOR

Like Edmund, Jasper was given a title (Earl of Pembroke), lands, and acted as an advisor to Henry VI in regard to Wales. He remained loyal to Henry VI and the Lancastrian cause until his death. He raised his nephew, the future Henry VII, and was instrumental in putting him on the throne. Jasper and Henry VII spent years trying to stay one step ahead of the Yorkists who sought to get rid of the remaining Lancastrian threat, AKA Henry VII. He married Catherine Woodville who was Elizabeth of York's (Henry VII's wife and Queen) maternal aunt; however, he had no legitimate children and never acknowledged any illegitimate children, if he had any.

## HENRY VI

Henry VI proved to be an ineffective ruler, especially in comparison to his father, Henry V, and his rival, Richard, Duke of York. He married Margaret of Anjou in a failed effort to end the Hundred Years' War and they had one son, Edward of York. His ultimate downfall was his mental instability, which he likely inherited from Catherine's side of the family (her father was called the Mad King, after all). Richard and the Yorkists rebelled against him, and Margaret led the Lancastrian forces on Henry VI's behalf. The Yorkists won the first section of the war, despite Richard's death. Edward IV, Richard's heir, took the throne and imprisoned Henry VI in the Tower of London for the remainder of his life. While he was restored to the throne briefly, his mental state had declined significantly, and he was little more than a puppet. Edward IV reclaimed the throne and Henry VI's only son, Edward of York, died in battle. Almost immediately, Henry VI "died" in the Tower of London. While never confirmed, it was highly likely that Edward IV had him killed as Henry VI posed a threat to the York dynasty.

### EDMUND BEAUFORT

Edmund married Eleanor Beauchamp and had ten children with her. He became one of Henry VI's favorites and Richard, Duke of York's, bitter rival. He took command of the troops in France at the end of the Hundred Years' War and lost key battles. He was rumored to be Edmund Tudor's father as well as Edward of York's (Henry VI's son) father. He had a very close relationship with Margaret of Anjou. He was one of the first major casualties of the War of the Roses.

# Appendix B

# Family Connections

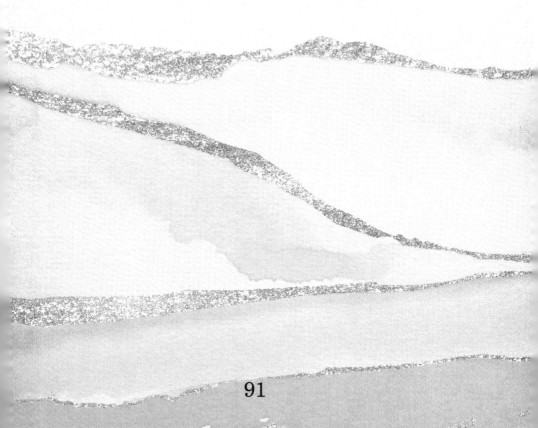

## CATHERINE OF VALOIS

| Birth | Death | Coronation |
|---|---|---|
| 27 October, 1401 | 2 January 1437 | 23 February 1421 |

## PARENTS

| Father | Mother |
|---|---|
| Charles VI of France | Isabeau of Bavaria |
| King of France | Queen of France |

## SPOUSES

| Henry V of England | Owen Tudor |
|---|---|
| King of England Lord of Ireland | Welsh Courtier |
| Married 1420-1422 | Married 1428-1437 |

## CHILDREN

| Henry VI of England | | |
|---|---|---|
| King of England<br><br>Disputed King of<br>France<br><br>Lord of Ireland | 1421-1471 | Married to<br><br>Margaret of Anjou |
| **Edmund Tudor** | | |
| Earl of<br>Richmond | 1430-1456 | Married to<br>Margaret Beaufort |
| **Jasper Tudor** | | |
| Duke of Bedford | 1431-1495 | Married to<br><br>Catherine Woodville |

## GRANDCHILDREN

| Edward of Westminster | | |
|---|---|---|
| Prince of Wales | 1453-1471 | Married to Anne<br>Neville |
| **Henry VII of England** | | |
| King of England<br><br>Lord of Ireland | 1457-1509 | Married to<br><br>Elizabeth of York |

## Siblings

| Isabella of Valois | | |
|---|---|---|
| Queen Consort of England<br><br>Duchess of Orleans | 1389-1409 | Married to<br><br>(1) Richard II of England from 1396-1399<br><br>(2) Charles, Duke of Orleans from 1406-1409 |
| **Joan of Valois** | | |
| Duchess of Brittany | 1391-1433 | Married to John V, Duke of Brittany |
| **Charles of Valois** | | |
| Dauphin of France | 1392-1401 | Never married |
| **Marie of Valois** | | |
| Prioress of the Convent of Poissy | 1393-1438 | Became a nun |

| | | |
|---|---|---|
| **Michelle of Valois** | | |
| Duchess of Burgundy | 1395-1422 | Married to Philip III, Duke of Burgundy |
| **Louis of Valois** | | |
| Duke of Guyenne Dauphin of France | 1397-1415 | Married to Margaret of Nevers |
| **John of Valois** | | |
| Duke of Touraine Dauphin of France | 1398-1417 | Married to Jacquline, Countess of Hainault, Holland and Zeeland |
| **Charles VII** | | |
| King of France | 1403-1461 | Married to Marie of Anjou |

# Appendix C

# Sources and Further Reading

Hilton, Lisa. Queens Consort: England's Medieval Queens from Eleanor of Aquitaine to Elizabeth of York. Pegasus Books. New York: 2021. Kindle Edition.

Jones, Dan. The Plantagenets: The Warrior Kings and Queens Who Made England. Penguin Random House LLC. United States of America: 2014. Kindle Edition.

Jones, Dan. The War of the Roses: The Fall of the Plantagenets and the Rise of the Tudors. Penguin Random House, LLC. United States of America: 2015. Kindle Edition.

Lawless, Erin. Forgotten Royal Women: The King and I. Pen and Sword Books Ltd. Yorkshire: 2019. Kindle Edition.

McGrigor, Mary. The Sister Queens: Isabella &
Catherine de Valois. The History Press:
2016. Kindle Edition.

Weir, Alison. The War of the Roses. The
Random House Publishing Group. New
York: 1995. Kindle Edition.

# Acknowledgements

Thank you to my amazing and supportive family (Dave, Cindy, Matt, and Katie) for editing this over and over again.

Thank you to my friends and family who dealt with my crazy while I made this happen.

# About the Author

K. Lee Pelt, otherwise known as "the Snarky History Nerd", fell in love with stories at a young age. She was always reading and coming up with stories in her head. As she got older, the love of stories expanded to a love of history, which, in many ways, is one giant story from many different perspectives. After completing her Bachelor of Arts in Medieval European History, she went on to get a Masters of Education. K. Lee utilizes her degrees to tell the stories of history, especially those of women, with a snarky twist.

When she is not writing, you can find K. Lee watching TV (usually some form of comedy or snarky drama) or reading everything from fanfiction to history books to romance novels with her cat, Noelle, climbing all over her.

# Note from the Author

Thank you so much for taking the time to read about one of my favorite English Queen Consorts, Catherine of Valois. I hope you enjoyed reading it.

**I would greatly appreciate it if you would:**

*Review this book.* This helps authors immensely. So if you liked this book and are willing to, please submit a review on Amazon.

*Share this book:* If you like this book, please share it with your friends, either in person or across social media. This will help tremendously.

*Connect with me:* I would love to chat with anyone about Medieval history. You can email me at thesnarkyhistorynerd@gmail.com or connect with me through social media. My social media information is in the "Stay Tuned..." Section.

Stay tuned...

The next book in the works is on Elizabeth of York, another fantastic Queen Consort. You can keep up to date on all things Snarky History Nerd, including release dates and blog posts, by following me on social media or checking out my website. The details are below:

Website: snarkyhistorynerd.com

Twitter: @ snarky_history

TikTok: @kleepeltsnarkyhistory

Instagram: snarkyhistorynerd

Facebook Page: https://m.facebook.com/100086266522638/

Printed in Great Britain
by Amazon

26738143R00059